ANIMAL KINGDOM

ADULT COLORING BOOK

A HUGE ADULT COLORING BOOK OF 60 WILD ANIMAL DESIGNS IN A VARIETY OF STYLES AND DETAILED PATTERNS

D1313663

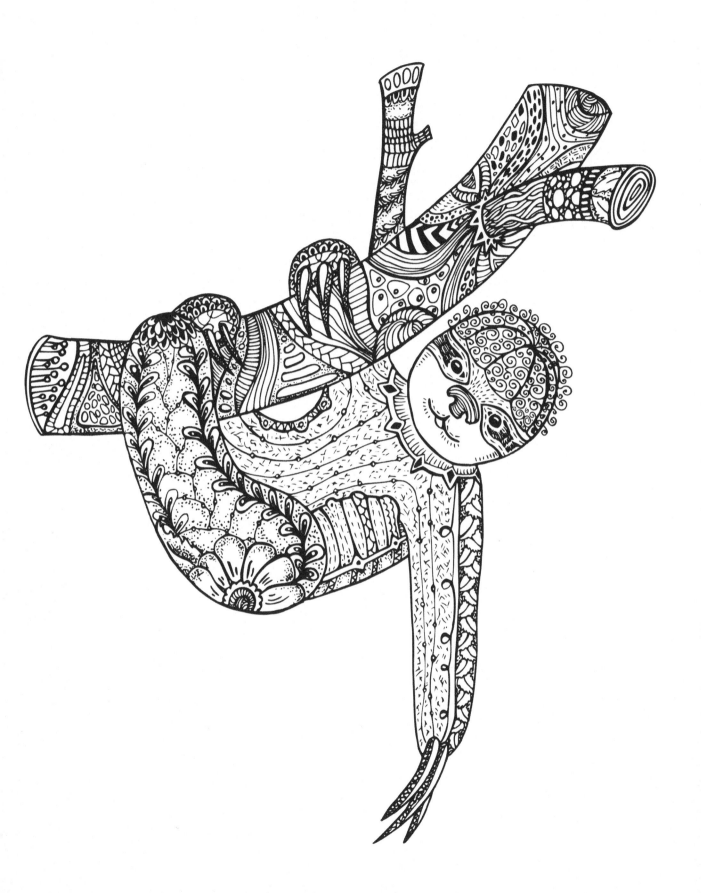

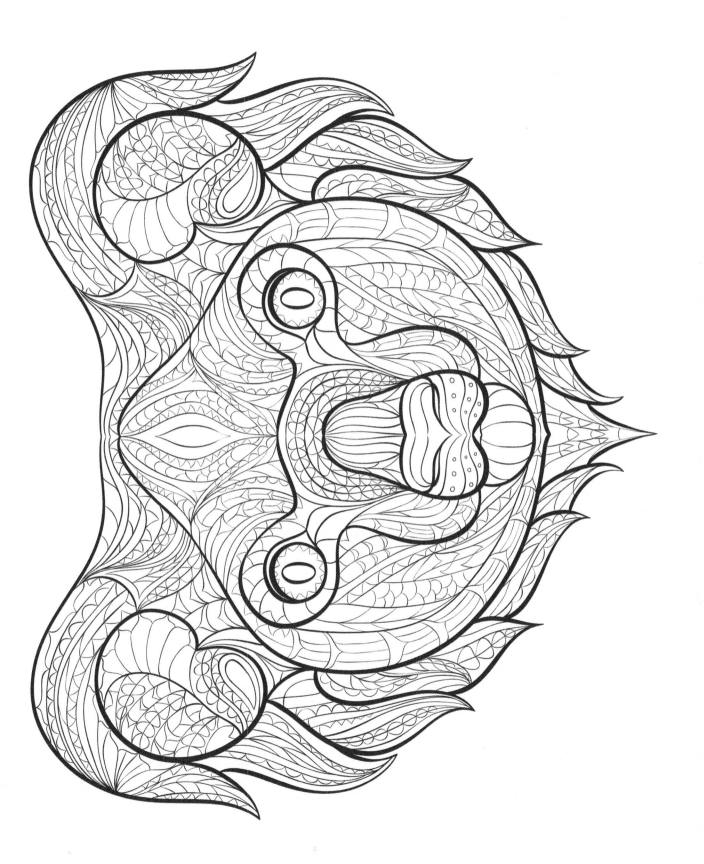

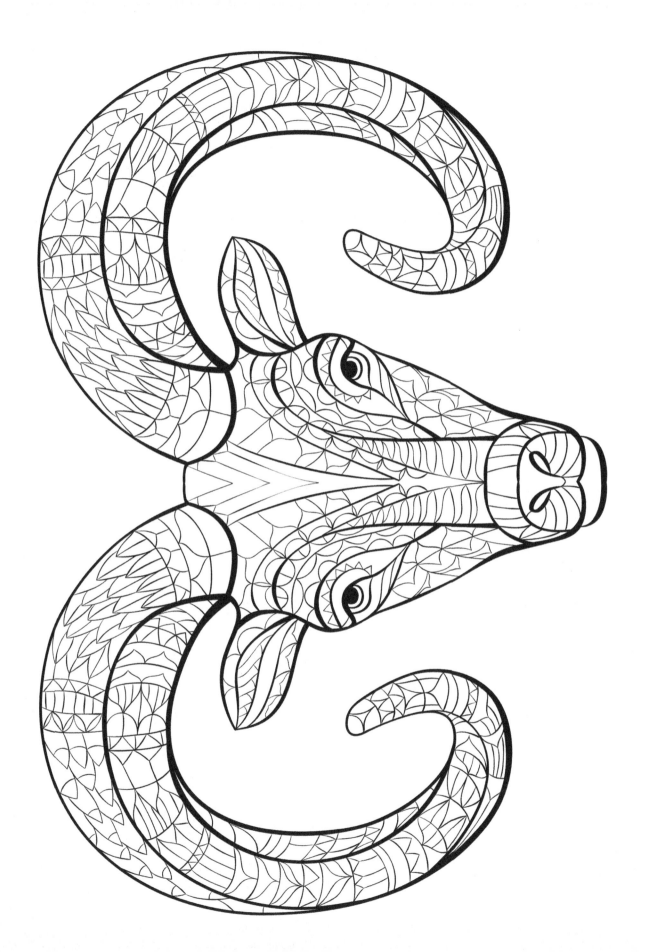

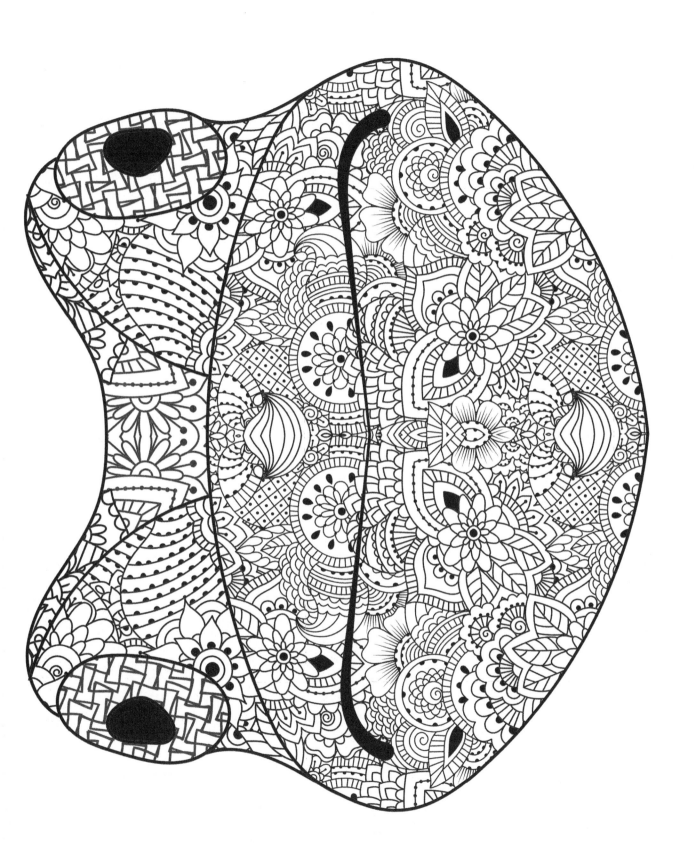

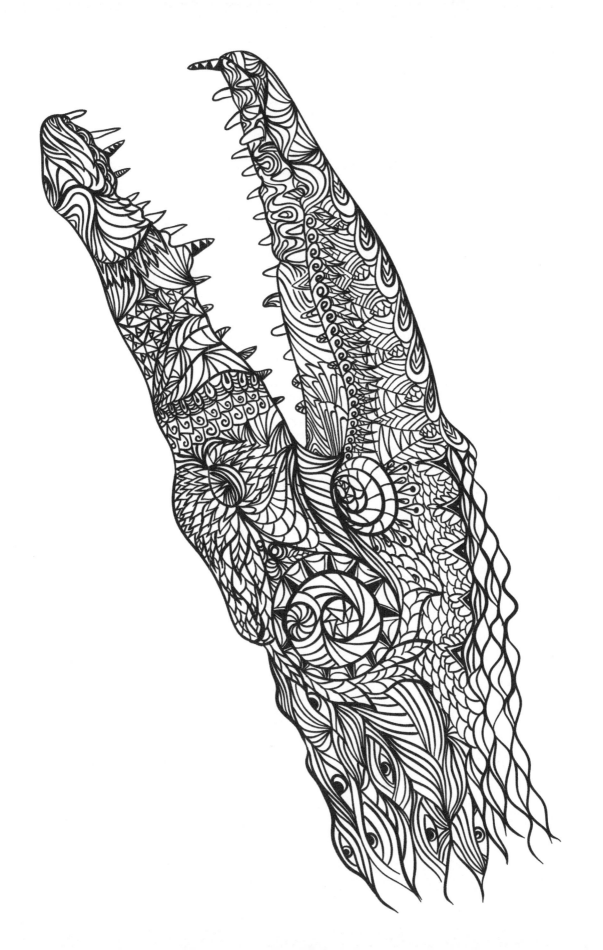

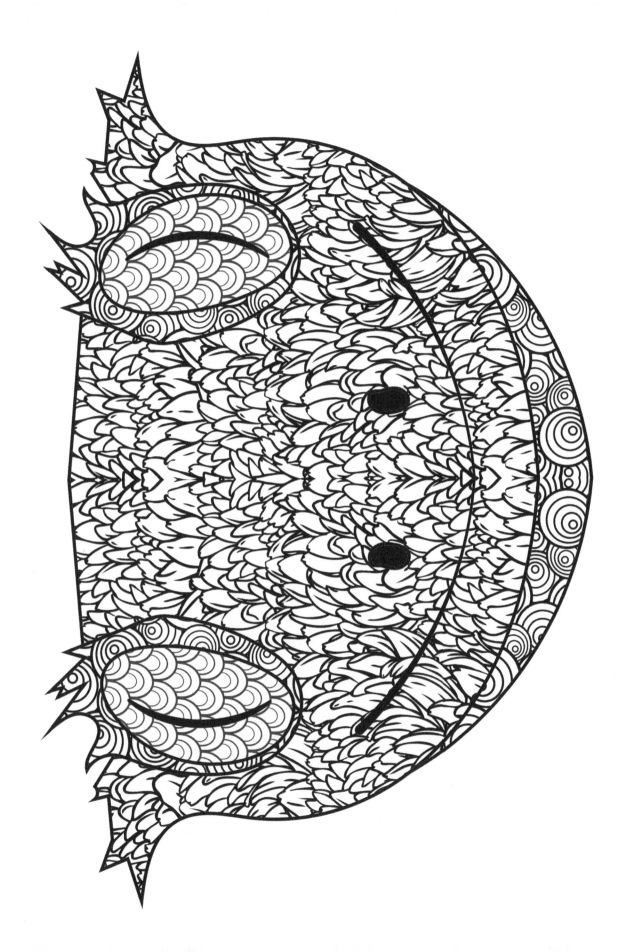

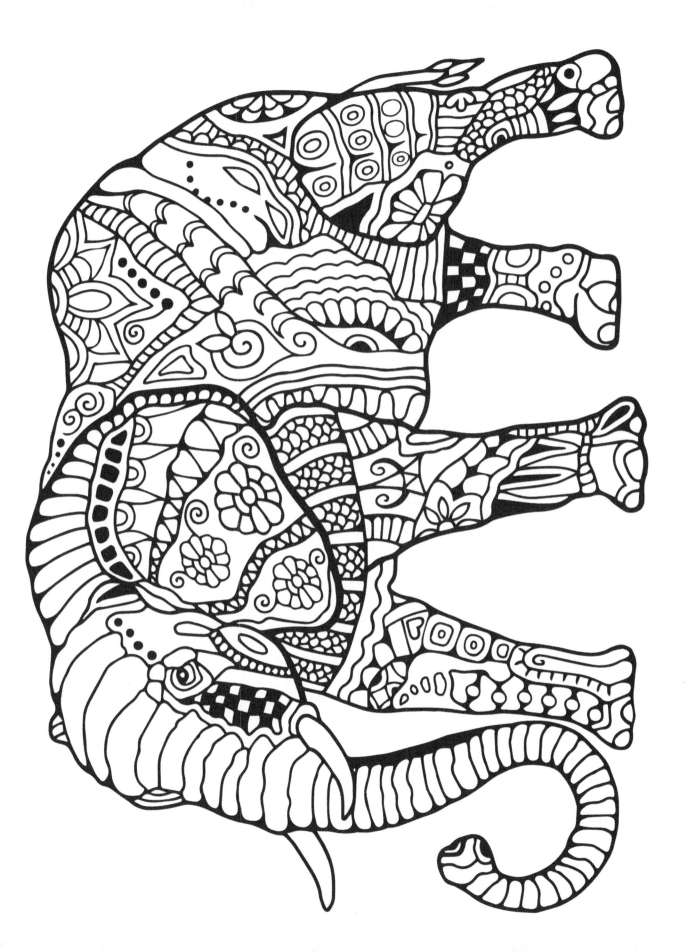

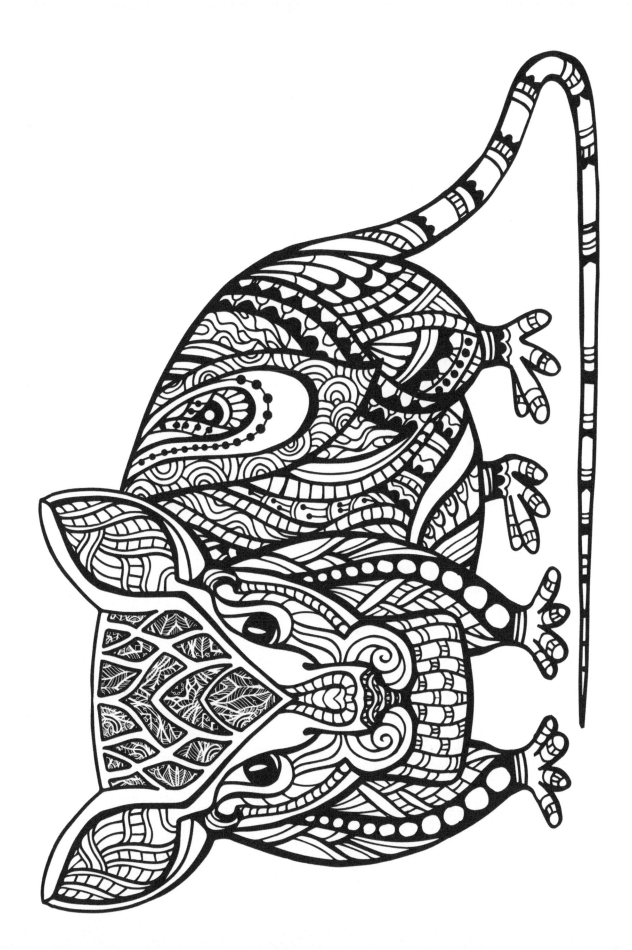

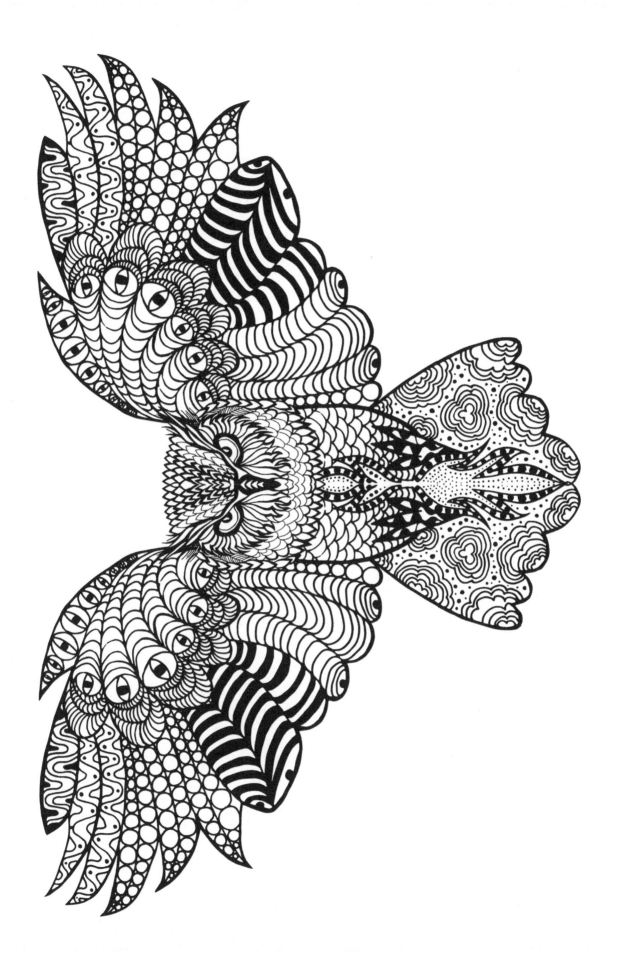

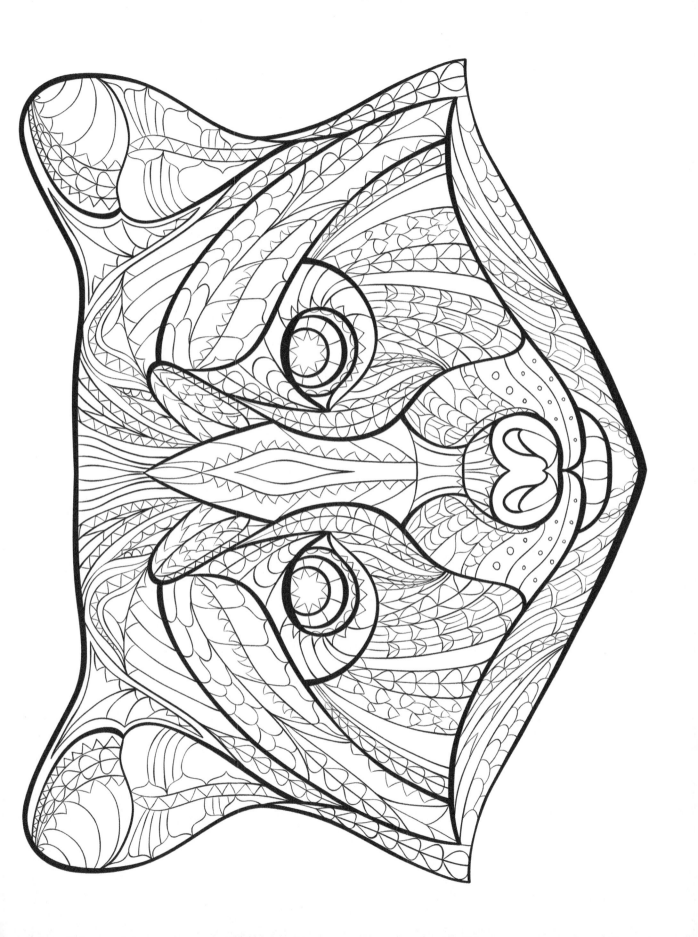

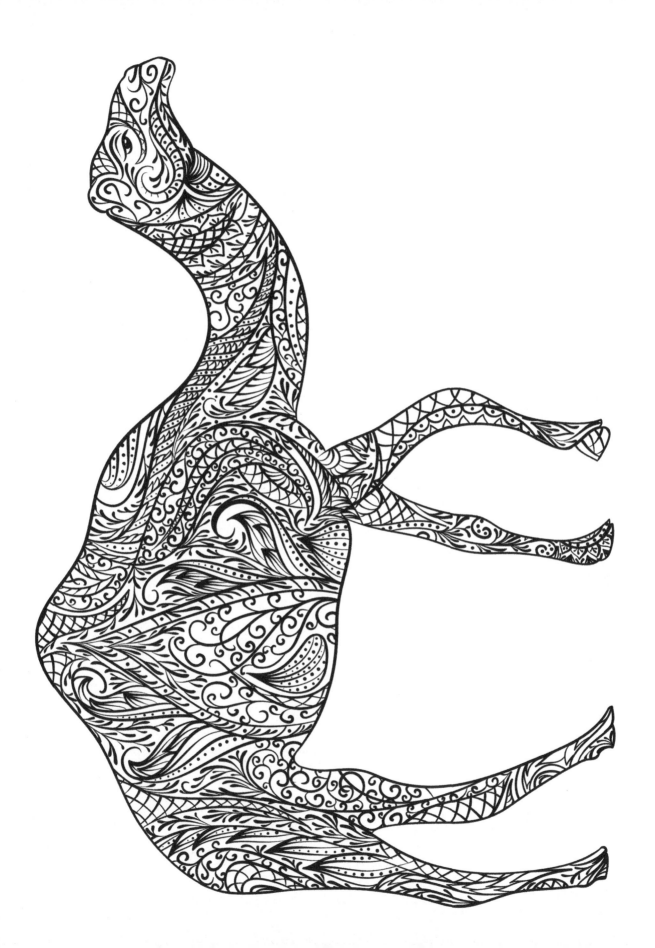

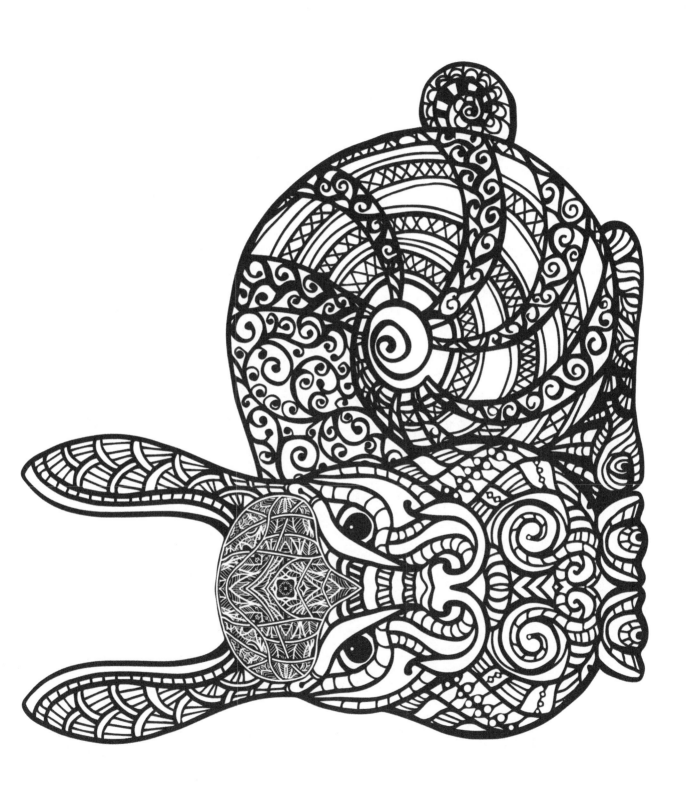

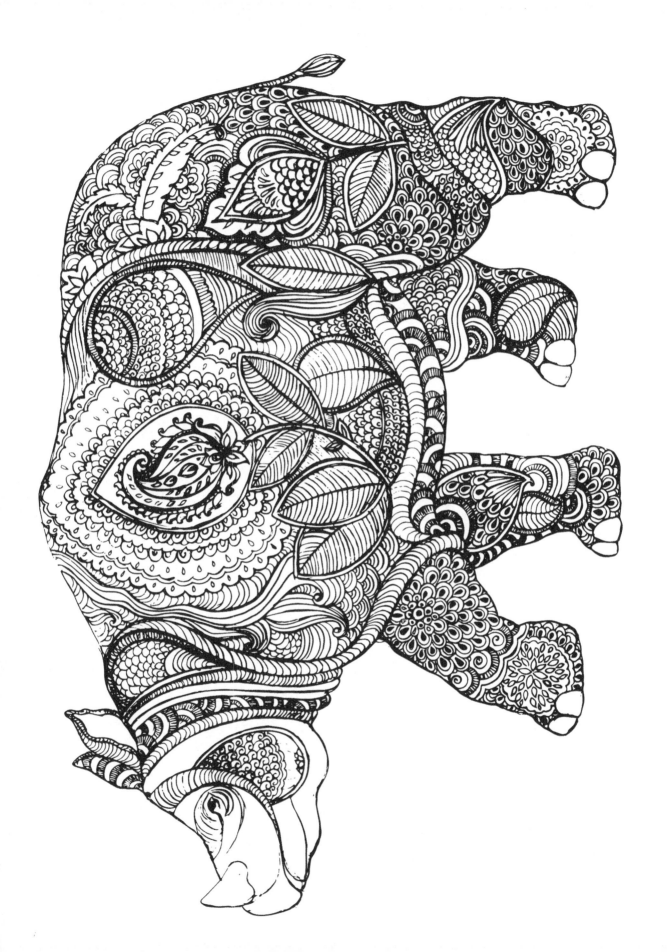

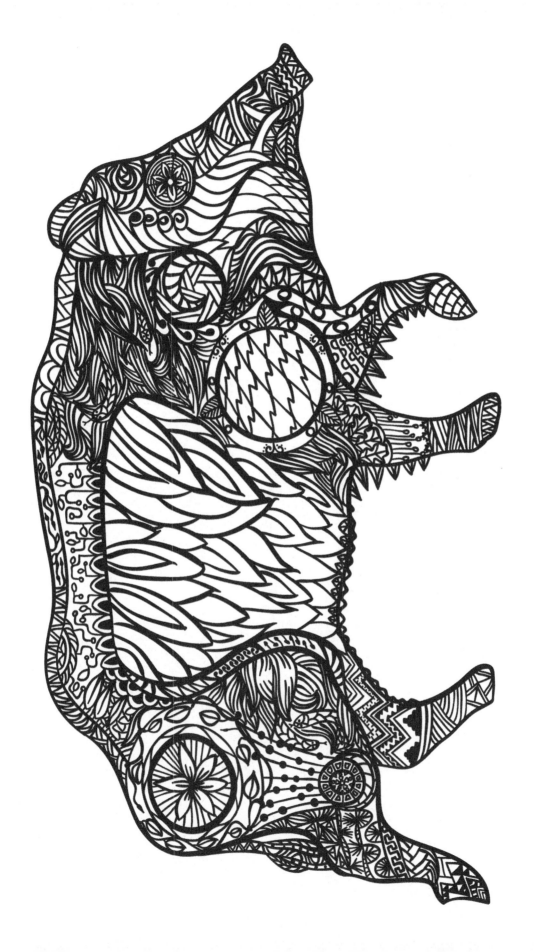

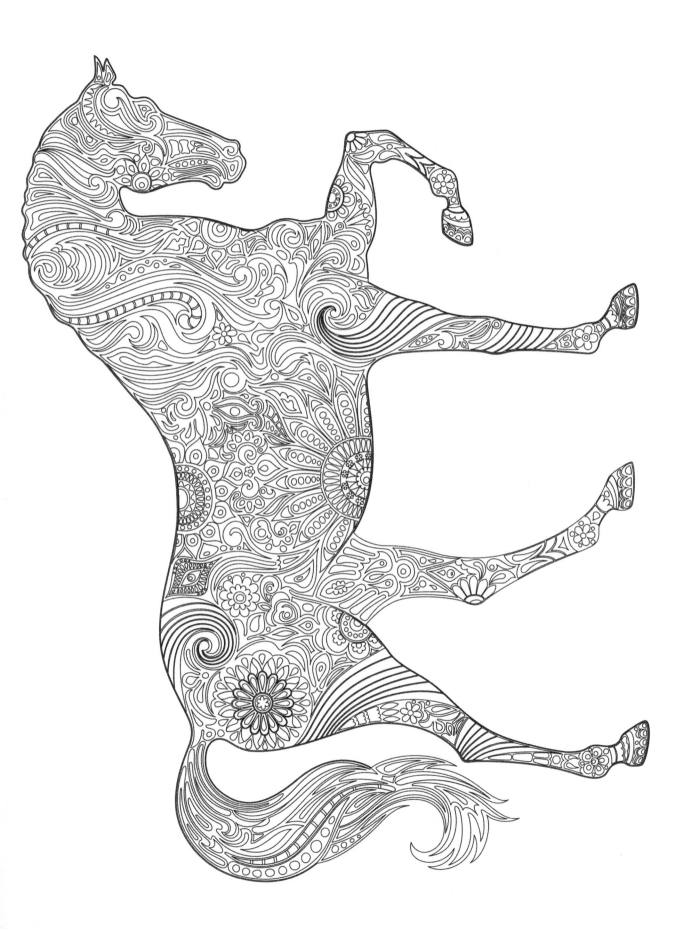

Made in the USA
Las Vegas, NV
03 May 2023

71483008R00070